BLACK COUNTRY
DICTIONARY
& PHRASE BOOK

STEVE EDWARDS

**Dedicated to Ava and Harrison
(My Black Country children)**

CONTENTS

The Black Country

The Black Country is a region in central England. Geographically, it encompasses either the whole or part of each of the four Metropolitan Boroughs of Dudley, Sandwell, Walsall and Wolverhampton.

The Black Country was at the heart of the industrial revolution. For as far as the eye could see, coal mines and coking works, iron foundries and forges, glass factories and brickworks dominated the landscape. The air pollution caused by all these industries is believed by many to be the reason the region is called the Black Country. Soot and smoke bellowing from chimneys and furnaces polluted the air to such an extent that daylight hours were darker than night-time. The Black Country was described as 'Black by Day and Red by Night' as the glow from furnaces lit the night-time sky.

In 1832, 13-year-old Princess Victoria's coach passed close to the region now known as the Black Country. In her diary, she wrote, "I just now saw an extraordinary building flaming with fire. The country continues black, engines flaming, coals in abundance. Every where, smoking and burning coal heaps."

The Black Country Dialect

Black Country 'spake' is often criticised and mocked by people from outside the area. Black Country folk are told to 'speak proper English.' In fact, we do speak 'proper English'. The traditional Black Country dialect preserves many archaic traits of Early Modern English and even Middle English.

My grandad Fred (Edwards) would frequently use the words 'Thee' for 'you' and 'Thine' for 'yours.' He'd ask 'Ow B'ist,' meaning "How are you?"

In actual fact, Black Country People speak English in its most original form. So, the next time someone questions our Black Country English, be sure to inform them that "we dun spake propa."

Yam Yam

No guide to Black Country Dialect would be complete without mentioning the term Yam Yam.

Our near neighbours, the good people of Birmingham claim the credit for coining the term. It is how they like to refer to us Black Country folk. They're quite proud of inventing a clever a little name for us that succeeds in taking the Mickey out of the way we speak.

But typical of the famous Black Country sense of humour, rather than get shirty with the Brummies or see the term as offensive, we embraced it. We're proud to be Yam Yams!

You see, instead of saying 'you are" we say "yow am." That is almost always shortened to "yow'm." And when said in normal Black Country conversation, to the untrained ear it sounds like "Yam." Here's an example.

- Normal English. "You're crazy but you're still my friend."

- Black country dialect. "Yow'm nuts but yow'm still mah mairt."

- Sounds like. "**Yam** nuts but **yam** still mah mairt."

Black Country Phrases

After speaking to hundreds of local characters, I have compiled a list of phrases and sayings that Black Country People use.

Some are sayings I remember my grandparents using which are rarer today, but most of the phrases and sayings are still very much in use.

Now we all know Black Country dialect is easier to speak than to read. A good tip is to read each individual word first then say the whole sentence quickly. In this guide the phonetic sound "aah" rhymes with noise a sheep makes "baah."

So, to our friends from outside the Black Country feel free to use this guide to learn our lingo. As for those of you fortunate enough to be born and bred in the Black Country, here's your chance to brush-up on the language of home. Or perhaps you could test your mom or dad to see how many they remember. Or you might want to simply read and smile as you let these lovely phrases take you on a trip down Memory Lane and evoke memories of your grandparents.

BLACK COUNTRY PHRASE BOOK

Ya fairtha wannts ya.	Your father wants you.
Goo an mytha ya nan.	Go and bother your grandmother.
Shut ya cairk'ole.	Shut your mouth.
Theer's aahr ode mon.	There's my dad.
He come umm kaylied.	He came home drunk.
E day gerrin till squalin time.	He didn't get in until the early hours.
Weer's er gone?	Where has she gone?
Er's blabberin with er mairts.	She is talking with her friends.
Yow'm wuss then me.	You're worse than me.
Ar'll goo fust.	I will go first.
Me missis is a nuss.	My wife/girlfriend is a nurse.
Them goozgogs gid me the bally airk.	Those gooseberries have given me the belly ache.

Cloze the gairt.	Close the gate.
Ar'll ate me dinna lairta.	I'll eat my dinner later.
Mate an tairtas for tay.	Meat and potatoes for tea.
Dairv's on is oss aggen..	Dave is on his horse again.
Iss rairnin aggen	It's raining again.
Er's like a glede under a doowa.	She has a terrible singing voice.
Er ooss t'be a chairnmekka.	She used to be a chainmaker.
Yower turn t'do the claynin.	Your turn to do the cleaning.
Av a look in me puss.	Have a look in my purse.
Ar'm caggy'onded.	I am left handed.
On th'otha ond.	On the other hand.
Dun ya wannt opple?	Do you want an apple?
Thuz sum stew in the pon.	There is some stew in the saucepan.

Weem gooin up the bonk	We are going up the bank.
E 'ud do summat like tha.	He would do something like that.
Well, Ar'll goo t'the foot of our stairs.	Well, I never, that's surprised me.
Well, Ar'll goo t'Brahl'ill. (Brierley Hill)	Well, I never, that's surprised me.
Yow've med a codge o' tha.	You have made a poor job of that.
Ar'll giv yow a cog-winda.	I will give you punch.
Woss the crack?	What are we doing?
Woss up wi yar fairce?	Why do you look so moody? (what is up with your face?)
Iss black over the back o'Bill's mother's.	A big storm is brewing.
Ar bay a Brummie.	I am not from Birmingham.
Thay dow like we.	They don't like us

Thass ers'n an thass is'n.	That one's hers and that one's his.
Thass ow'rn.	That one is ours.
Er went all round the reekin. (Wrekin)	She gave a long-winded explanation before getting to the point.
Er went all round the reekin. (Wrekin)	She travelled the longest route imaginable to get to her destination.
Ar've knowed im f'donkey's 'ears.	I've known him a long time.
Ode Ears Night.	New Year's Eve.
Wonn yow wannt?	What do you want?
Wonn yow gunna do abaaht it?	What are you going to do about it?
Mah feet'm code.	My feet are cold.
Them two 'ud spile anotha couple.	Those two are perfectly suited.
Er's ad a lickle chap.	She has had a baby boy.
Er's ad a lickle wench.	She has had a baby girl.

The babby's a blaahtin.	The baby is crying.
Yow core goo in theer.	You can't go in there.
Thee cosn't goo in theer.	You can't go in there.
Ar've lost me kay.	I have lost my key.
This ay gerrin the babby wasshed.	We're not getting the job done sitting here.
Ow am ya?	How are you?
Ow bist?	How are you?
Ow bin ya?	How are you?
Ar've ad a bost-up wi' them next doowa.	I've been arguing with the neighbours
Me an ya fairtha's ad a big bost-up.	Your dad and I have had a huge row.
Ar've sid er afowa.	I've seen her before.
Dow do tharaggen.	Don't do that again.
Ar've gorra yed airk.	I've got a head ache.
Are, Ar'll av some fittle.	Yes, I will have some food.
I ay ad 'em.	I haven't had them.

Ar've bin t'Dugley.	I have been to Dudley.
It 'it im on the bonce.	It hit him on the head.
Er's bost er tie.	She has broken her toy.
We ad a bostin time.	We had a very good time.
They'm from Brummagem.	They are from Birmingham.
Ar catched the buz.	I caught the bus.
Mutha's a-cantin aggen.	Mother is gossiping again.
Ar'll av a catlick.	I will have a quick wash.
Get ya chops round tha.	Eat that.
Santa comes daahn the chimdy.	Santa comes down the chimney.
Woss yow chunterin about?	What are you grumbling about?
Yow saft clarnet.	You daft fool.
Ar'm clammed.	I am hungry.
Put ya coot on, iss code aaht.	Put your coat on, it's cold out.

Am yow a-cootin?	Do you have a boyfriend/girlfriend?
Ar day do it .	I didn't do it.
Dow do tha.	Don't do that.
Ar'll av a dollop of tha.	I will have some of that.
Wassh yer donnies.	Wash your hands.
Dow drap it.	Don't drop it.
Wull yow goo t'the shap?	Will you go to the shop?
Juss sharrap.	Just shut up.
Them fakes'ull kill ya.	Those cigarettes will kill you.
Thas sum bostin fittle.	That is some great food.
Wassh ya fizzog.	Wash your face.
Gooin t'the flics.	Going to the cinema.
Workin in the fode.	Working in the back yard.
Dow worry, Ar've fun it.	Don't worry, I have found it.
Yow ay very gairn.	You are not very capable.

Thass me gammy leg.	That is my poorly leg.
Woss you gawkin at?	What are you looking at?
Woss yow gorrin ya gob?	What do you have in your mouth?
Mom, 'e chucked arf-enda at me.	Mum, he threw a brick at me.
The wammel's jed.	The dog is dead.
Ar wow be a jiffy.	I won't be long.
Put the keckle on.	Put the kettle on.
Ar'll lamp yow in a bit.	I will hit you in a moment.
Goo an play on the lezzer.	Go and play on the field.
Yow'm onny a lickle bit ay ya?	You're only small, aren't you?
We ad a propa loff.	We had a proper laugh. (we had a good time)
Yow'll av a clip round the lug'ole.	You will have a clip around the ear.
Warro, me ode mucka.	Hello, my old friend.
I ay got nairun.	I haven't got one.

Ar dow wannt nayther on 'em.	I don't want either of them.
Ow ode'm yow?	How old are you?
Gi me th'omma.	Pass me the hammer.
E ood do summat like tha.	He would do something like that.
Th'ode ooman next doowa.	The old woman next door.
Ar'll pail yow if yow dow sod off.	I will beat you up if you don't leave me alone.
Dun yow wannt a piecey?	Do you want a sandwich?
They'm pikelets.	They are crumpets.
Er's podged the queue.	She has jumped the queue.
Ar puk up a fiva.	I picked up five pounds.
Thass riffy.	That is dirty.
Yow'm cowin saft.	You are stupid.
Yow bay right.	You are stupid.
Smosh tharegg f'me.	Break that egg for me.

Thez a pida on the sailin'.	There is a spider on the ceiling.
Oi, thass mah sate.	Excuse me, that is my seat.
Er's as wicked as a wasp.	She's in a bad mood, beware.
Av yow done me snap?	Have you done my food for work?
Gorrenny suck?	Have you got any sweets?
Tararabit.	Goodbye.
Av yow gorrenny tairtas?	Have you got any potatoes?
Tek the wammel wi' ya.	Take the dog with you.
Yow tek afta ya mutha.	You resemble your mother.
That'n ull do.	That one will be ok.
Thissen's betta then yarn.	This one is better than yours.
Weege one'm yowers?	Which ones are yours?

Gerrit dahn ya wassin.	Get it down your throat. (Eat or drink something)
Come eya, me wench.	Come here, my girl.
Ar'll see yow the wickend.	I will see you the weekend.
Ar'm gooin wum.	I am going home.
We'm gooin fishin daahn the cut.	We are going fishing down the canal.

The Black Country Alphabet

'A' is for 'Opple

'B' is for 'Narna

'C' is for 'Council pop

'D' is for 'Donnies

'E' is for 'Ere ya goo!

'F' is for 'Fittle

'G' is for 'Giz a goo!

'H' is for 'Oss'

'I' is for 'Ickle

'J' is for 'Jed

'K' is for Kaylied

'L' is for Loike

'M' is for Mucker

'N' is for Nah

'O' is for Ow am ya?

'P' is for Tairta

'Q' is for Quid

'R' is for Riffy

'S' is for Suck

'T' is for Tara a bit

'U' is for Umm

'V' is for Vest

'W' is for Ooman

'X' is for Kiss

'Y' is for Yampy

'Z' is for Stripy oss

Apple. Banana. Tap-water. Hands. Here you go. Food.
Can I have a go? Horse. Small. Dead. Drunk. Like. Friend.
No. How are you? Potato. Pound. Dirty. Sweets.
Good Bye. Home. Vest. Woman. Kiss. Daft. Zebra.

The Black Country Alphabet
Designed by Black Country T-shirts.

BLACK COUNTRY DICTIONARY

A	
Aahr Bin Ya?	How are you?
Aahr bist?	How are you?
Aer Kid	My brother
Arf bairked	Dopey
Aloone	Alone
An'all	As well
Any road up	Anyway
Ar bay	I'm not
Ar bin	I am
Ar cor	I can't
Are	Yes
Ark!	Listen!
Ay?	Pardon?
Ay	Haven't, isn't, aren't

B	
Back'onda	Slap with the back of the hand
Back'uds	Backwards
Baggies	West Bromwich Albion
Barfe	Vomit
Bargie	Canal boatman
Barny	Disagreement
Bay	Not
Bibble	Small stone/pebble
Big yed	Arrogant person
Bin Yow	Are You
Blaaht	Cry
Blabbrin' on	Talking silly
Bladder	Balloon
Blathered	Drunk
Bloke	Man

Bob-owla	A big moth
Boff	Flatulence
Bonk	Hill
Bost	Broken
Bostin	Very good
Bost-up	Big argument
Brevittin	Rumaging
Brahl'ill	Brierley Hill
Brummidgem/Brumagem	Birmingham
Buz	Bus
C	
Caggy'onded	Left handed
Cairk'ole	Mouth
Cantin	Gossiping or chatting for a long time
Chate	Cheat
Chobble	To crunch sweets/scratchings

Chookin	Throwing
Chuffed	Happy
Clack	Tonsils
Clammed	Very hungry
Clarnit	Daft person
Claynin the crocks	Washing the dishes
Clobba	To hit someone
Conk	Nose
Coot	Coat
Cor	Can't
Craird'leath	Cradley Heath
Crairdlee	Cradley
Crookid	Grumpy
Cuffy	Scruffy
Cut	Canal
D	
Daahn	Down

Donkey's 'ears	Long time
Donny	Hand
Dobbin	Wheelbarrow
Doolally	Insane
Doowa	Door
Daaht the light	Turn off the light
E	
'E	He
'Ears	Years
'Er	Her / she
F	
Faggits'n Pays	Faggots and Peas
Fairce	Face
Fairk/Fake	A Cigarette
Fairtha	Father, Dad
Ferritin	Trying to find something
Fickle	Food

Filch	Steal
Fittle	Food
Fizzog	Face
Flerta	Catapult
Fode	Back Yard
Fortnit	Two week period
Fowa	Four
Franzy	Grumpy
Fust	First
G	
Gab	Gossip
Gaffa	Boss
Gannit	Greedy eater
Gawk	Look
Gawp	Mouth open
Gerrin	Get in.
Gid	Gave or Given

Gizzit ere	Give it to me
Gledes	Embers in a coal fire
Gob	Mouth
Gooin	Going
Goozgog	A gooseberry
Gorrit	Got it
Grizzle	To cry pathetically without tears.
Grorty Dick	Groaty Pudding
Guzzlin	Drinking fast
H	
Ham	A Black Country person trying to talk posh. "how ham ya?"
Hisn	His
Hum	Home
I	
'Is	His

It ay arf	It certainly is
Iyul	Oil
J	
Jammy	Lucky
Jed	Dead
K	
Kayford	Kingswinford
Kaylied	Drunk
Kid	Child
Kiddie	Kidderminster
Kite off (to)	To run away
L	
Lampin'	Thrashing, beating
Larrupped	Drunk
Leg it	Run
Lezzer	Field
Loffin	Laughing

M	
Mairt	Mate, Friend
Mardy	Moody
Mate	Meat
Med	Made
Mek	Make
Mekshift	Temporary
Miffed	Upset
Mind yow	Although
Missis	Wife
Mom	Mum - Mother
Mon	Man
Mont	Bad mood
Mooch	Looking for something
Moowa	More
Mucka	Friend
Muggins	Fool

Munch	Kiss and hug small child or baby

Gizza a munch of 'im |
Mytha	Pester
N	
Nah	No
Narna	Banana
Ninkampoop	Fool
Nit nuss	Visiting school nurse who inspects for head lice
Nizgul	Stupid person
Noo	New
Nuss	Nurse
O	
Ode	Old
Ode 'ill	Old Hill
Odebree	Oldbury
Offal	Cheap Meat

'Omma	Hammer
On yer bike!	Go away
'Ond	Hand
Ooman	Woman
Op 'n a catch	Now and again
Opple	Apple
Oss	Horse
Oss Road	Street
Ow do	Hello
P	
Pairstin	Beating
Pays	Peas
Piece a cairk	Easy
Piecies	Sandwiches
Pinny	Pinafore/Apron
Pither	Potter around aimlessly
Poke	A stye on the eyelid

Puddled	Daft, crazy
Puss	Purse
Q	
Quarry Bonk	Quarry Bank
R	
Razza	Reservoir
Riffy	Filthy
Ronk	Smelly
Rot	Rat
S	
Saft	Daft
Scrumpin'	Stealing apples
Scurf	Dandruff
Shap	Shop
Sharra	Coach
Sharrap	Shut up
Sheeding	Spilling

Skivvy	A servant
Sling yer 'ook!	Go away!
Smerrick	Smethwick
Smosh	Break into bits
Smoshin	Good, Great "We ad a smoshin time"
Sozzled	Drunk
Spake	Speak
Sponna	Spanner
Sprog	Child
Spug	Chewing Gum
Staahbridge	Stourbridge
Stick wood in th'ole	Shut the door
Suck	A sweet
Suck	Some sweets
Suff	Drain
Summat	Something

T	
Taahn	Town
Tackybonk	slag heap
Tairta	Potato
Tar	Thank you
Tat	Rubbish
Tatta	Someone who collects scrap metal
Tay	It isn't
Tay	Cup of Tea or an afternoon meal
Thairn	Theirs
The Renna	Wren's Nest Housing Estate
Thee	You
Thee cosn't	You can't
Th'utha	The other
Thrairpin	Good hiding
Tiddla	A small fish or a small item

Tie	Toy
Tittybabby	Cry-baby or Wimp
Tipp'n	Tipton
Tod	On your own "On yer tod"
Took 'is 'ook	He's gone
Towellin'	Beating
Traa ra-bit	Goodbye
Tranklements	Bits and pieces
U	
Umm	Home
Uwa!	Ouch
W	
Wairta	Water
Wallop	Hit
Wammel	Dog
Warro	Hello
Wassp	Wasp

Wassh	Wash
Wazzin	Throat
Wench	Girl
Werret	An irritating child,
Wik	Week
Woe	Won't
Wolvo	Wolverhampton
Wore	Wasn't
Wuddslee	Wordsley
Wum	Home
Wust	Worst
Y	
Yampy	Barmy
Yarn	Yours
Yed	Head
Yow am	You are
Yowern	Yours

Yow	You
Yow'll	You will
Z	
Zonked aaht	In a deep sleep.

Message from the Author.

Thank you for reading the Black Country Dictionary and Phrase Book. I hope you had as many loffs reading it as I did writing it.

If I've left out any of your favourite Black Country words or phrases, please let me know by visiting propablackcountry.co.uk

Steve Edwards.